curious about

MCDONALD'S

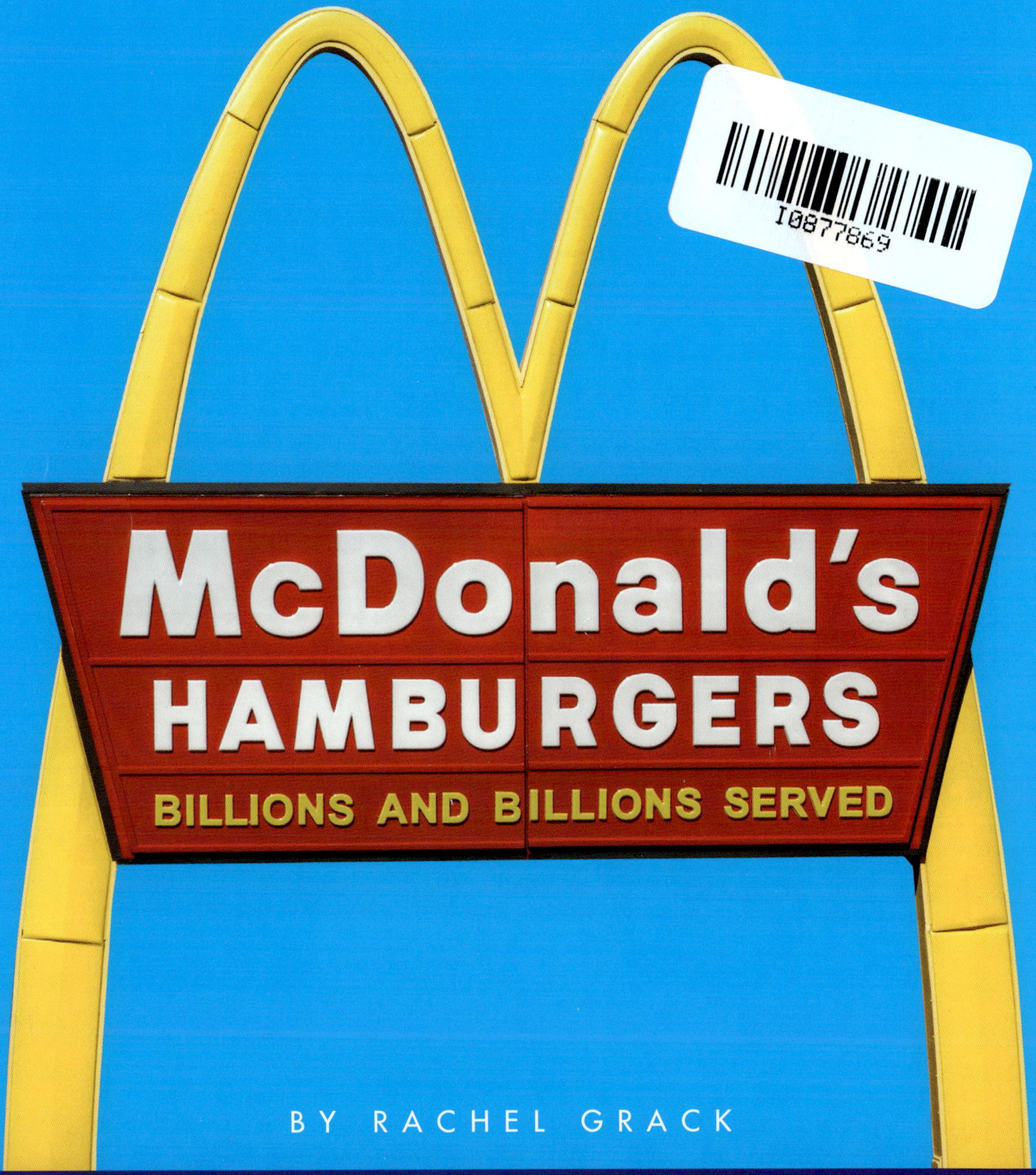

BY RACHEL GRACK

AMICUS LEARNING

What are you

CHAPTER ONE

McDonald's McStart

PAGE 4

CHAPTER TWO

Under the Arches

PAGE 8

curious about?

CHAPTER THREE

Bet You Didn't Know...

PAGE

18

Stay Curious! Learn More . . .22

Glossary 24

Index 24

Curious About is published by
Amicus Learning, an imprint of Amicus
P.O. Box 227, Mankato, MN 56002
www.amicuspublishing.us

Editors: Ana Brauer and Grace Cain
Series Designer: Kathleen Petelinsek
Book Designer and Photo Researcher: Sara Hood

Library of Congress Cataloging-in-Publication Data
Names: Koestler-Grack, Rachel A., 1973–author.
Title: Curious about McDonald's / by Rachel Grack.
Description: Mankato, MN : Amicus Learning, an imprint of Amicus, [2026] | Series: Curious about favorite brands | Includes bibliographical references and index. | Audience: Ages 6–9 | Audience: Grades 2–3 | Summary: "Who founded McDonald's? Spark elementary readers' curiosity about the popular fast food brand's history, products, and cultural impact with insightful questions and well-researched answers. Includes table of contents, glossary, further resources, and index"— Provided by publisher.
Identifiers: LCCN 2024050044 (print) | LCCN 2024050045 (ebook) | ISBN 9798892005111 (library binding) | ISBN 9798892005654 (paperback) | ISBN 9798892006194 (ebook)
Subjects: LCSH: McDonald's Corporation—Juvenile literature. | McDonald's Corporation—Miscellanea. | Fast food restaurants—Juvenile literature. | Fast food restaurants—Miscellanea.
Classification: LCC TX945.5.M33 K64 2026 (print) | LCC TX945.5.M33 (ebook) | DDC 338.7/616479573—dc23/eng/20250110
LC record available at https://lccn.loc.gov/2024050044
LC ebook record available at https://lccn.loc.gov/2024050045

Photo Credits: Alamy Stock Photo/BirchTree, 2, 13, Everett Collection, 7, Robert Landau, 2, 5; Getty Images/Samir Hussein, 17, Scott Olson, 14–15, Tim Boyle, 6; Shutterstock/ATIKAN PORNCHAIPRASIT, 9, DFree, 17, Fred Duval, 17, Jonathan Weiss, cover, 1, kckate16, 10–11, Lenscap Photography, 18, makalex69, 16, Patcharaporn Puttipon4289, 19, Viktor_IS, 3, 20–21; The Noun Project/Daniel Llamas Soto, 22, Isabel Foo, 22, Made, 23, Miftah, 23; Wikimedia Commons/Gage Skidmore, 17, McDonald's, 8, McDonald's Corporation, 8, Steve Jurvetson, 17

Every effort has been made to contact copyright holders for material reproduced in this book. Any omissions will be rectified in subsequent printings if notice is given to the publisher.

Printed in India

CHAPTER ONE

When did McDonald's open?

In 1940. The first McDonald's was in California. The owners were Dick and Mac McDonald. It was a drive-in barbecue restaurant. People parked their cars and waited for a **carhop**. The server took their orders. He brought food back to the car. This was the start of the famous food **brand**.

The oldest operating McDonald's opened in 1953. It is in Downey, California.

The first McDonald's menu only had nine items.

Did McDonald's invent fast food?

No. White Castle was the first fast food chain. It had a small, simple menu. This made service faster. The McDonald brothers liked the idea. In 1948, they invented the Speedee Service System. It was like an **assembly line** for making food. Orders were ready within minutes.

DID YOU KNOW?
Salesman Ray Kroc (right) bought the company in 1961. He turned McDonald's into a fast food chain!

CHAPTER TWO

2

What are the Golden Arches?

They are McDonald's famous **logo**. The first stores had one arch over each end of the building. The parking lot sign also had one on top. Travelers easily noticed the bright yellow lights. In 1962, the arches were doubled to look like an M.

MCDONALD'S LOGO OVER TIME

McDonald's FAMOUS BARBECUE

1940

McDONALD'S FAMOUS HAMBURGERS BUY'EM BY THE BAG

1948

McDonald's®

1953

McDonald's®

1961

McDonald's®

1975

1993

The arches are meant to catch your eye.

When did McDonald's add a drive-thru?

In 1975. It was near an army base in Sierra Vista, Arizona. Soldiers cannot wear their uniforms in public unless on duty. They must stay in their cars. So the store owner added a sliding window. Soldiers could drive up and order from their cars.

There are more than 25,000 drive-thrus worldwide.

How many McDonald's are there?

Over 40,000! They serve millions of people every day. They can be found all over the world. And thousands of new restaurants open every year. The United States alone has more than 13,000 locations. You don't have to travel far to find one.

DID YOU KNOW?
Houston, Texas has more McDonald's than any other city in the world. Take your pick from 126 stores!

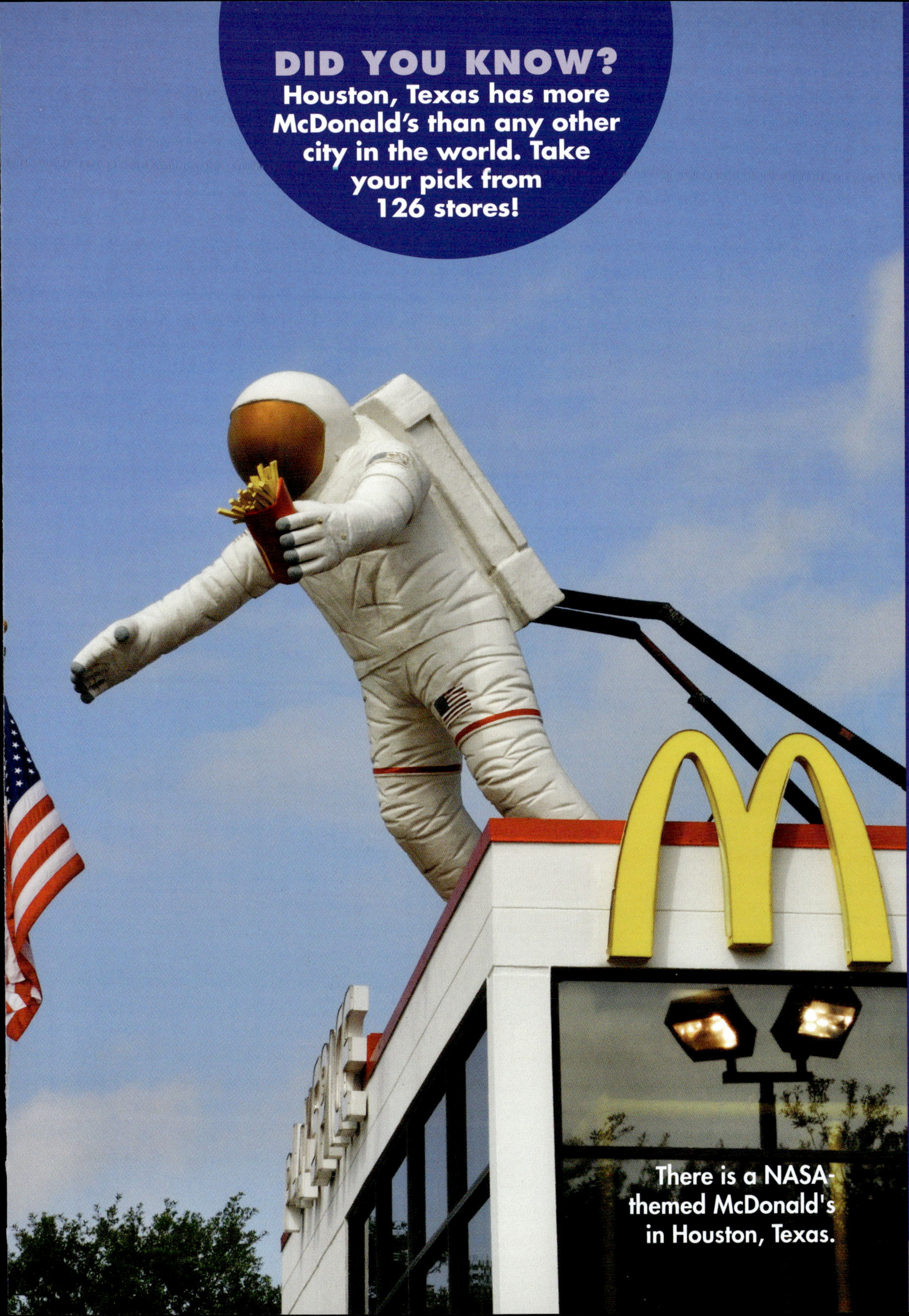

There is a NASA-themed McDonald's in Houston, Texas.

CosMc's™
Order He

What is CosMc's?

It is a McDonald's spin-off. It started in 2023. It is a big drive-thru. There are no tables or chairs inside. Grab an iced coffee, fruit drink, or boba tea to go. Snack on breakfast sandwiches, pretzel bites, or McPops donut bites.

As of 2025, there are six CosMc's locations in the US.

Could I work at McDonald's?

McDonald's workers are called "the crew."

Sure! But you must be at least 14 years old to apply. McDonald's is a great place to work. The company also offers **tuition** assistance. Your job could help pay for college. McDonald's is a popular first job for many people. Even some famous people have worked there!

P!NK
SINGER AND SONGWRITER

MARK HAMILL
ACTOR,
STAR WARS MOVIES
(1977–1983, 2015–2019)

JEFF BEZOS
FOUNDER OF AMAZON

RACHEL MCADAMS
ACTRESS,
DOCTOR STRANGE (2016),
MEAN GIRLS (2004)

LIN-MANUEL MIRANDA
ACTOR AND SONGWRITER,
HAMILTON (2015)

CHAPTER THREE

Who invented Happy Meals?

The Happy Meal box was designed by Bob Bernstein.

Good question! In the mid-1970s, Yolanda Cofiño, a manager in Guatemala, came up with the idea for a kids' menu. In 1977, Bob Bernstein came up with the name Happy Meal. Each box includes a toy. The toys are often popular characters such as Hello Kitty.

About 5,000 Happy Meals are sold every minute.

The McDonald's characters are often in the Macy's Thanksgiving Day Parade.

Who are the McDonald's characters?

DID YOU KNOW?
In 1974, McDonald's opened the Ronald McDonald House Charities. They provide a place to stay for families with children in the hospital.

Popular characters include Ronald McDonald, the Hamburglar, and the Fry Kids. But Grimace is the most popular today. Believe it or not, he is supposed to be a giant taste bud. And that's what McDonald's is all about. Yummy food!

STAY CURIOUS!

ASK MORE QUESTIONS

How many McDonald's are in my city?

How does McDonald's make a difference?

Try a BIG QUESTION: How much fast food is safe to eat?

SEARCH FOR ANSWERS

Search the library catalog or the Internet.
A librarian, teacher, or parent can help you.

Using Keywords
Find the looking glass.

Keywords are the most important words in your question.

If you want to know about:

- the number of McDonald's in your city, type: MCDONALD'S IN (YOUR CITY)
- how McDonald's makes a difference, type: MCDONALD'S COMMUNITY

LEARN MORE

FIND GOOD SOURCES

Here are some good, safe sources you can use in your research.
Your librarian can help you find more.

Books

McDonald's
by Kaitlyn Duling, 2020.

Ray Kroc
by Mary Nhin, 2021.

Internet Sites

McDonald's Animated History
https://www.youtube.com/watch?v=ygM3DFucj5o
Watch a short video highlighting McDonald's history.

McDonald's Family Fun Hub
https://www.mcdonalds.com/us/en-us/family-fun-hub.html
The Family Fun Hub is an interactive site with online books, games, and art printables.

Every effort has been made to ensure that these websites are appropriate for children. However, because of the nature of the Internet, it is impossible to guarantee that these sites will remain active indefinitely or that their contents will not be altered.

SHARE AND TAKE ACTION

Compare prices.
How much was food at your favorite McDonald's when it first opened?

Research different McDonald's buildings.
Find the strangest and the fanciest ones.

Draw a new McDonald's character.
Share your creation with your friends.

GLOSSARY

assembly line A series of workers who each perform a job to put something together.

brand A group of products owned by the same company.

carhop A server who takes orders at a car window and brings the food back to the car.

charity An organization that helps people in need.

logo A picture or symbol that stands for a company.

tuition The fee for instruction at a college or university.

INDEX

arches, 8–9

Bernstein, Bob, 18, 19

characters, 19, 20–21

Cofiño, Yolanda, 19

CosMc's, 15

crews, 16, 17

drive-ins, 4

drive-thrus, 10–11, 15

fast food, 6–7

Houston, Texas, 13

Kroc, Ray, 7

McDonald brothers, 4, 6

Ronald McDonald House
Charities, 21

About the Author

Rachel Grack has been editing and writing children's books since 1999. She lives on a small ranch in southern Arizona. As a lover of stories, Disney is close to her heart. She also enjoys watching her grandchildren play Pokémon games on her Nintendo 64 console.